IN A WORLD OF TEARS AND SORROW

100 intercessory poems to guide prayer and inspire reflection

NICK FAWCETT

kevin mayhew

kevin mayhew

First published in Great Britain in 2018 by Kevin Mayhew Ltd
Buxhall, Stowmarket, Suffolk IP14 3BW
Tel: +44 (0) 1449 737978 Fax: +44 (0) 1449 737834
E-mail: info@kevinmayhew.com

www.kevinmayhew.com

© Copyright 2018 Nick Fawcett

The right of Nick Fawcett to be identified as the author of this work has been asserted by him in accordance with the Copyright, Designs and Patents Act 1988. All rights reserved.

All rights reserved. No part of this publication may be reproduced, stored in a retrieval system, or transmitted, in any form or by any means, electronic, mechanical, photocopying, recording, or otherwise, without the prior written permission of the publisher.

9 8 7 6 5 4 3 2 1 0

ISBN 978 1 84867 938 2
Catalogue No. 1501570

Cover design by Rob Mortonson
© Image used under licence from Shutterstock Inc.
Typesetting by Angela Selfe

Printed and bound in Great Britain

To all the unsung people who faithfully lead intercessions each week or who strive in ways large and small to change this world for the better.

Contents

About the author   8
Introduction   9

Disaster, times of
1. Another drought, another war   13
2. Catastrophe has struck again   14
3. The storm has wreaked its havoc   15
4. To those who face disaster   16
5. Tragedy again, Lord   17
6. Where wind and rain have battered   18

The environment
7. Broken and despoiled   21
8. Can we see the ice caps melting   22
9. Logging in the jungle   23
10. Our planet's faced with crisis   24
11. Think about this planet   25
12. What riches we have on this planet   26

Faith in action
13. Did you hear my plea when I called you?   29
14. I cannot change the world alone   30
15. I hate your songs of worship   31
16. I hear of human hunger   33
17. If you'd truly worship   34
18. Reach out in love if you would follow me   35
19. There's too much hurting, too many tears   36
20. We talk of love and friendship   37
21. When I groaned with hunger   38

Health and sickness

22.	For all those who've been injured	43
23.	Hear our prayer for doctors	44
24.	Lord, thank you for our senses	45
25.	We pray for those who suffer	46
26.	When summer years have ended	47
27.	With love, let us remember	48

Loneliness

28.	If you're feeling sad and lonely	51
29.	No one comes to see them	52

Loving others

30.	A group of thieves were waiting	55
31.	A rich man came seeking	56
32.	Are you hungry?	57
33.	God gives a new commandment	58
34.	In the poor and broken	59
35.	It's easy to speak about love	60
36.	Someone near is hurting	61
37.	Will you open your hand to the hungry?	62
38.	You say that you would love me?	63

Poverty and human need

39.	Can you spare a penny?	67
40.	Do you know what it's like to be lonely?	68
41.	Do you see the children	69
42.	Have you seen the vagrant	70
43.	Spare a thought for someone	72
44.	When they turned me from your borders	74

Prejudice and discrimination

45.	The world is cruelly broken	77
46.	We claim to be enlightened	78

Questions of faith

47.	I saw a loved one die today	81
48.	I try to keep on trusting	82
49.	The world, it seems, is full of pain	84
50.	We talk of a God who loves us	85
51.	Why do you turn away, Lord?	86

Relationships

52.	If a friend's in need and you just don't care	89
53.	Let us do to others	90
54.	Stop finding fault with others	91
55.	There's nothing quite like laughter	92
56.	When I fail to be the person	93
57.	When someone shows a little act of kindness	94
58.	When you're feeling bruised and battered	95

Service

59.	Can I be of service?	99
60.	Can I give assistance?	100
61.	For those who give their money	101
62.	For those who work to keep us safe	102
63.	If you're hurting	104
64.	Let us serve one another	106
65.	Will you offer service?	107

Social justice

66.	A voice is calling, somewhere	111
67.	Falsehoods are spoken	112
68.	I hear the sound of bitter weeping	113
69.	In a world where all too many	114
70.	In this world of markets	115
71.	'Is there no one there to hold me?'	116
72.	Let us work together	118
73.	Someone in the world is hungry	119

74.	Someone's anxious, someone's fearful	120
75.	Think about the things you buy	121

Sorrow and trouble

76.	For all oppressed by sorrow	125
77.	For all those facing testing	126
78.	For the anxious, fearful	127
79.	For the sick and dying	128
80.	For those for whom the path is steep	129
81.	No words express sufficiently	130
82.	We greet each day alight with joy	131
83.	Where there's loss – the gall of sorrow	132

War and peace

84.	Did you spy my tears in the news shot?	135
85.	God of every nation	136
86.	God of the nations	137
87.	Our world is scarred by madness	138
88.	Tell me that you've heard about the tears we've shed	139
89.	Though we come from different places	140
90.	When tensions are livid, suspicions are strong	141

World need

91.	For all who wander far from home	145
92.	In a world of tears and sorrow	146
93.	In a world of trouble	147
94.	In a world where countless people	148
95.	Picture a world without any hatred	149
96.	Someone's weeping, someone's sobbing	150
97.	Stop a while and listen	152
98.	Voices are crying	153
99.	What fate awaits our children?	154
100.	Where innocents still suffer	155

About the author

Brought up in Southend-on-Sea, Essex, Nick Fawcett served as a Baptist minister for thirteen years, and as a chaplain with Toc H for three, before deciding to focus on writing and editing, which he continues with today, despite wrestling with myeloma, an incurable cancer of the blood. He lives in Wellington, Somerset, with his wife, Deborah, and has two children, Samuel and Kate, the first now living in Exeter, the second at university in Manchester. Delighting in the beauty of the West Country, Nick and Deborah love nothing more than walking stretches of the South West coast path at weekends, and Nick – as well as finding time for online games of chess and Scrabble, and supporting local football teams Taunton and Tiverton Town, alongside his many editing commitments – finds constant inspiration for his numerous books in the lanes and footpaths near his house. His aim, increasingly, is to write material free of religious jargon that reaches out to people of all faiths and none.

Introduction

I have loved poetry since I was a boy at school, taking delight several times then at having one of my offerings published in the school magazine. There are, of course, two types of poems. There's what we term 'blank verse' – the format in which much classic poetry has been written – but there's also rhyming verse, which though sometimes sneered at by the cognoscenti has, I believe, equal power to move and inspire people, provided that the rhymes are natural and unforced. Such poems can speak in a way prose or blank verse does not, succinctly expressing a challenge and encouraging reflection.

Since the earliest days of my time in the pastoral ministry, I've also always been a great believer in intercessory prayer, not in any simplistic sense – ask God and he's sure to deliver – but convinced that concern for the wider world and issues of social justice are not just optional issues for the Christian or any other believer but integral to what faith is all about. Religion that turns in on itself has little to offer anyone. We need to pray for others, but we must recognise equally that this is never an end in itself. 'I'll pray for you,' we can too easily say, as though doing that is enough. It is not. True intercessory prayer stirs us into action, whether it be giving to charity, visiting the sick, comforting the bereaved and lonely, volunteering for a good cause, or simply showing someone that we care.

In this book I have brought poetry and intercession together as a resource for both public worship and personal devotion – it is equally suitable for either. Each poem is designed to stimulate thought, to stir the heart and call for a response. If you're using them in the context of public worship, you may choose to invite the congregation to listen in an attitude of quiet reflection, and afterwards to spend a short time in silent prayer. Alternatively, you may want to follow a poem with a more formal prayer, perhaps using one from my recent book *Intercessions for a Hurting World*, or using one of your own. Should you be using the poems for personal devotion, I'd urge reading each one slowly and thoughtfully, then spending a few moments quietly considering its meaning before committing the subject prayerfully to God.

It is my hope and belief that the material here can speak in a way that other prayers cannot quite capture, leaving the issues covered and needs prayed for fresh in the mind long after the words have first been heard, and helping to turn good intentions into action. If that proves so, the book will have been well worth the writing.

Nick Fawcett

DISASTER, TIMES OF

(*See also* Sorrow and trouble)

1.   Another drought, another war

Another drought, another war,
one more catastrophe;
another bomb, another death,
in perpetuity.

Another person dying young,
another tragic death;
another act of genocide
or murder linked to race.

Another nation left in debt –
still deeper poverty.
Another famine, harvest failed –
a fresh calamity.

Another case of child abuse,
of harassment and rape;
of people trapped in slavery
from which there's no escape.

It seems that nothing changes, Lord;
still less do things improve.
However much we beg you to,
you never seem to move.

Although faith seems a mystery –
we beg you: hear our prayer.
To all who face such misery,
reach out and show you care.

2. Catastrophe has struck again

Catastrophe has struck again,
lives thrown in disarray.
God, in the chaos, show your love
and offer help, we pray.

To those who mourn a loved one killed,
or home now swept away,
grant comfort in their time of need –
give help and strength, we pray.

To those with livelihoods destroyed
who cannot pay their way,
grant funds to help them build again –
give help and strength, we pray.

To those who seek to bring relief
and suffering allay,
grant the resources that they need –
give help and strength, we pray.

To those who strive to plan ahead
to keep such times at bay,
grant wisdom, guidance, diligence –
give help and strength, we pray.

3. The storm has wreaked its havoc

The storm has wreaked its havoc;
the clean-up's just begun:
a picking up the pieces –
such dreadful damage done.
A multitude bewildered,
their lives in disarray;
communities left broken
and loved ones swept away.

To all who offer shelter
and all who reassure;
to those who in the chaos
strive bravely to restore;
to everyone affected
and struggling to get through –
rekindle faith and vision
and help to make things new.

Give comfort to the grieving;
turn darkness into light.
Bring gladness after sorrow
and daybreak after night.
Reach out to those left reeling
and help them know you care.
Bring hope and help and healing,
Lord, hear us; hear our prayer.

4. To those who face disaster

To those who face disaster,
their world stood on its head;
communities in turmoil,
left burying their dead;
give comfort in their trouble,
support in their distress.
Though all for now seems hopeless,
bring solace nonetheless.

To those now deep in mourning
and those who fear the worst,
those traumatised and injured –
the many being nursed –
those searching in the chaos,
still daring to believe,
give strength and consolation –
their agony relieve.

To those confused and frightened,
uncertain where to turn;
those seeking news of loved ones,
their fate at last to learn;
Lord God, give reassurance,
the help they need to cope;
amid the devastation
give reason still to hope.

5. Tragedy again, Lord

Tragedy again, Lord,
leaves our world in pain;
countless lives in turmoil,
creaking with the strain.

Heartbreak hard to cope with,
worry tough to bear;
hope all but extinguished –
ousted by despair.

Many people injured;
many others dead;
multitudes unsure of
just what lies ahead.

Hundreds needing shelter,
food in short supply,
ravaged by diseases –
watching loved ones die.

Reach out in their trauma;
help, and hold, and heal.
Comfort, tend, encourage –
show your love is real.

Stir our hearts, in turn, Lord;
show us what to do.
Through our giving freely,
help them to get through.

6. Where wind and rain have battered

Where wind and rain have battered,
where people's lives are shattered,
where homes are torn and tattered,
bring hope, Lord God, bring hope.

Where families are grieving,
left numb and disbelieving
by blows beyond conceiving,
bring help, Lord God, bring help.

Where people still are dying,
their numbers multiplying,
despair intensifying,
bring strength, Lord God, bring strength.

Where multitudes are reeling
from that with which they're dealing,
the pain and shock they're feeling,
bring peace, Lord God, bring peace.

Where chaos brings confusion,
and hope seems an illusion,
religion a delusion,
bring faith, Lord God, bring faith.

THE ENVIRONMENT

(*See also* World need)

7. Broken and despoiled

Broken and despoiled,
pillaged and abused;
plunder of resources
carelessly excused;
earth stands at a crossroads,
future on the brink.
Will we try to mend things?
Will we stop to think?

Though we're still uncertain
what it all might mean,
will we just continue
as we've always been –
heedless of tomorrow,
living for today,
hoping all our problems
simply go away?

Spare a thought for others:
those who pay the price,
hit by changing climate –
melting polar ice;
those whose homes are flooded,
livelihoods destroyed,
or whose lands are barren –
now a dismal void.

Think about the birthright
those to come deserve:
countless priceless treasures
vital to preserve.
Earth stands at a crossroads,
future on the brink.
Will we try to mend things?
Will we stop to think?

8. Can we see the ice caps melting

Can we see the ice caps melting
and not even be concerned?
Experts speak of changing climate –
have we really still not learned?
Life on earth exists in balance,
each dependent on the rest,
those who prophesy disaster
do not make such threats in jest.

Can we see our planet pillaged –
creatures hunted, homes destroyed,
species lost to us forever:
so much gone we once enjoyed?
Can we simply shrug our shoulders,
claim there's nothing we can do?
Those who care can make a difference,
though our numbers may be few.

Faith that turns its back on nature,
looks to heaven instead of earth,
is a destitute religion,
wholly lacking any worth.
All of life on earth is precious,
held by us in sacred trust.
Stewardship is not some extra;
conservation is a must.

9. Logging in the jungle

Logging in the jungle;
hacking down the trees;
plastic in the ocean,
poisoning the seas;
soaring greenhouse gases;
toxic acid rain;
serve to put our planet
under mounting strain.

Dwindling resources
frittered in our haste;
swathes of land polluted;
coral reefs laid waste;
weather patterns changing:
storm and flood and drought.
Is there time to change things?
Will we work it out?

So much that is precious,
now we stand to lose.
We must grasp the nettle –
cannot pick and choose.
If we just continue
as we have before,
trouble and disaster
surely lie in store.

Think of other people,
those in other lands.
How we live affects them:
do not wash your hands.
Think of what God's given,
held by us in trust.
We can make a difference;
not just *can* but *must*!

10. Our planet's faced with crisis

Our planet's faced with crisis,
its future under threat,
as daily we exploit it
and leave its needs unmet.

We pillage and pollute it
with scarce a second thought.
Our greed obscures our duty
to tend it as we ought.

Like lemmings to a river,
like moths before a light,
we plunge towards disaster,
to never-ending night.

We say it will not happen,
that life will come up trumps,
and so go on consuming,
while filling rubbish dumps.

We claim we'll meet the challenge,
that somehow we'll get through,
but whether that's an option
depends on me and you.

The world's entrusted to us,
a treasure to maintain –
not just a tool for quenching
our greedy thirst for gain.

If we will just respect it,
it has so much to give.
Consider then your lifestyle;
reflect on how you live.

11. Think about this planet

Think about this planet.
Think about its health.
Celebrate its bounty.
Contemplate its wealth.
Gifts so very precious
are not ours alone,
but for our successors,
children not yet grown.

Think about tomorrow,
not just of today.
Don't abuse resources –
fritter them away.
Think about the footfall
that you leave behind;
how the world is slowly
being undermined.

Think about pollution,
poisoning our seas,
rivers, oceans, cities,
people, creatures, trees.
Call for better practice;
fight for cleaner air.
Change can be effected
if we really care.

If we live more simply
more may simply live,
each allowed their share of
what this world can give.
Care, then, for creation,
help conserve it all.
It's no fringe obsession
but a sacred call.

12. What riches we have on this planet

What riches we have on this planet,
what wonders surround us each day,
a dazzling spectrum of life-forms,
an awesome and diverse array.
A canvas of oceans and rivers,
of mountains and gullies and vales,
of meadows and gardens and wetlands,
of heathlands and forests and dales.

Yet though it may fill us with wonder,
we fail to ensure that it thrives.
We waste and abuse the resources
on which we depend for our lives.
We live with no thought of tomorrow,
ignore what we'd rather not face,
denuding our planet much faster
than nature can hope to replace.

Forgive, Lord, our folly, and blindness
to what this will cause us to lose;
our failure to think of our children,
to selflessly walk in their shoes.
Inspire a deeper commitment
to all you have placed in our care,
and help us ensure, in the future,
that others its riches may share.

FAITH IN ACTION

(*See also* Service)

13. Did you hear my plea when I called you?

Did you hear my plea when I called you?
In the lonely, the broken, the poor?
In the frail and the weak?
Those whose life is so bleak?
In the people afflicted by war?
Did you suffer their pain
as they cried out in vain?
Did you seek to respond to their need?
Did you feel their despair?
Ever show that you care?
Or complacently pay them no heed?

Did you hear my cry when I called you?
When I asked you to reach out and serve?
Were you able to see
that the call came from me?
Did my challenge perhaps hit a nerve?
Did your ears maybe burn?
Did you show your concern
at injustice, oppression and wrong?
Did you note what I said,
or ignore it instead,
and guiltily hurry along?

Did you hear my voice when I called you?
In the sobs of the hungry child?
In the pain and the fears
or the shedding of tears
of the outcast, despised and reviled?
Did you check these things out?
Did you bother about
helping anyone other than you?
If the world is to feel
that commitment is real
you must care about others too.

14. I cannot change the world alone

I cannot change the world alone,
I can't make all things new.
Beside the breadth of human pain
there's little I can do.
But I can show compassion,
and from my plenty share,
and through the things I do and say
can simply show I care.

I can't respond to every voice
or give to every cause.
I cannot heal the world's divides
or put a stop to wars.
But in a host of little ways
I still can play my part;
can work for peace and harmony –
responding from the heart.

I cannot make injustice end,
the poor and hungry feed.
I can't make evil disappear
or answer every need.
But I can join with others
in tackling what is wrong;
alone we can do little –
together we are strong.

15. I hate your songs of worship

I hate your songs of worship,
I loathe your words of prayer.
I count them so much rubbish –
you will not find me there.
Let's see your actions tally
with who you claim to be.
Let justice like a river
flow down and fill the sea.

You bring me your believing;
you put your creeds on show;
you argue over doctrine,
but I don't want to know.
Let's see your actions tally
with who you claim to be.
Let justice like a river
flow down and fill the sea.

You bring your busy programmes,
your meetings, fairs and fetes,
but these mean nothing to me:
they're merely empty dates.
Let's see your actions tally
with who you claim to be.
Let justice like a river
flow down and fill the sea.

You offer your commitment,
acknowledge me as Lord,
but all your protestations
will simply be ignored.
Let's see your actions tally
with who you claim to be.

(Continued overleaf)

Let justice like a river
flow down and fill the sea.

You think that works don't matter,
that faith is all you need,
but do not be complacent:
I simply won't take heed.
Let's see your actions tally
with who you claim to be.
Let justice like a river
flow down and fill the sea.

16. I hear of human hunger

I hear of human hunger,
of those who long for bread,
but though I mean to help them,
I help myself instead.
Although the spirit's willing,
the flesh is all too weak.
I fail to make a difference;
to do the good I seek.

I hear of war and bloodshed,
of broken refugees,
of camps where people huddle
in squalor and disease,
I ponder a donation,
and really mean to give,
but serving self deflects me
from helping others live.

I hear about injustice,
of countries racked by debt.
I say that I'll remember,
but always I forget.
Instead, I'm weak and greedy;
too prone to hesitate.
I turn my back on others,
and leave them to their fate.

I hear your voice, Lord, calling,
yet look the other way.
Instead of truly caring,
I simply say, 'I'll pray.'
Forgive my poor commitment
and help me play my part.
Give faith that shows in action;
transform my selfish heart.

17. If you'd truly worship

If you'd truly worship,
if you'd truly pray,
if you want to please me,
walk, then, in my way.
Many call me 'Master',
many call me 'Lord',
yet the frail and needy
daily are ignored.

If you'd truly serve me,
if you'd make me glad,
help to feed the hungry,
reach out to the sad;
strengthen those in trouble;
fortify the weak;
comfort those who suffer –
truth and justice seek.

If you want to follow –
my disciple be –
fight against oppression,
set my people free.
Pious words come cheaply,
deeds ask rather more.
Work against unfairness;
stand up for the poor.

Never be complacent,
trusting faith alone.
Words and deeds are partners –
lacking on their own.
You may call me 'Master',
you may call me 'Lord';
if such claims are empty,
you will be ignored.

18. Reach out in love if you would follow me

Reach out in love if you would follow me,
prove that you'd truly my disciple be,
care for the weak, and share with those in need,
bind up the wounds of those who hurt and bleed.

Give to the poor, bring hope in their despair,
labour for justice, demonstrate you care;
tend those who suffer, strive to bring relief;
share with the sorrowful, help bear their grief.

If you would truly serve me as you say,
walk in my footsteps, steadfast in my way;
put others first and seek the good of all,
then you will show you've understood my call.

19. There's too much hurting, too many tears

There's too much hurting, too many tears,
too many burdens, too many fears,
too much hunger, and too much need,
too much injustice . . . too much greed.

There's too much sickness, too much despair,
too much misfortune, too few who care,
too much anger and too much pride,
too many broken . . . deep inside.

There's too much envy, too much hate,
too many people left to their fate;
too much killing – what's it all for? –
too much division . . . too much war.

We can't work wonders, right every wrong,
solve every problem – we're not that strong –
can't do magic, or brandish a wand;
but what we *can* do . . . is respond.

The world needs healing, making anew.
It starts with people like me and you.
Hear them crying. What can we give?
How can *I* help them . . . help them live?

20. We talk of love and friendship

We talk of love and friendship,
how genuinely we care;
we boast about our closeness –
a special bond we share.
But is there any substance
behind the oaths we make?
Or are they glibly spoken
and easier to break?

We claim to live for others,
to care about the poor;
to gladly give a little
that others may have more.
But is there real intention
behind the words we speak?
Or is our caring hollow
and our commitment weak?

We claim to live for others,
to put the stranger first,
to see the best in people
where others see the worst.
Yet are we any different
in what we do and say?
Does anything about us
speak of a different way?

No one will pay attention
to anything we teach
unless we are consistent
and practise what we preach.
Fine words come all too cheaply,
yet are just so much air,
unless we show in action
how much we really care.

21. When I groaned with hunger

When I groaned with hunger,
how did you reply?
Did you try to feed me
or leave me there to die?
Have you yet not grasped it?
Do you still not see?
What you do for others
you do as well for me.

When I craved for water,
overwhelmed by thirst,
did you seek to slake it;
to save me from the worst?
Have you yet not grasped it?
Do you still not see?
What you do for others
you do as well for me.

When I battled sickness,
did you hear my call?
Did you try to comfort
or even care at all?
Have you yet not grasped it?
Do you still not see?
What you do for others
you do as well for me.

When I needed clothing,
did you heed my pleas?
Were you swift to answer
or still down on your knees?
Have you yet not grasped it?

Do you still not see?
What you do for others
you do as well for me.

When they held me captive,
tried to silence me,
did you work for justice,
attempt to set me free?
Have you yet not grasped it?
Do you still not see?
What you do for others
you do as well for me.

HEALTH AND SICKNESS

(*See also* Sorrow and trouble)

22. For all those who've been injured

For all those who've been injured –
the damage done severe –
deprived by what they've suffered
of much they once held dear;
their life now overshadowed
by harm beyond repair,
Lord God, for all such people,
we ask you, hear our prayer.

For those who've been assaulted,
left cruelly scarred for life
by acid or by beating,
by bullet or by knife;
now traumatised and broken,
lives haunted by despair,
Lord God, for all such people,
we ask you, hear our prayer.

For soldiers left disabled,
the casualties of war,
their life so very different
from what it was before;
adjusting to a challenge
at first too hard to bear,
Lord God, for all such people,
we ask you, hear our prayer.

For people racked by illness –
a shadow of the past.
For those who greet each morning
unsure if it's their last.
For all those facing treatment
they fear they cannot bear,
Lord God, for all such people,
we ask you, hear our prayer.

23. Hear our prayer for doctors

Hear our prayer for doctors,
in the work they do:
making diagnoses,
helping patients through,
offering their counsel,
healing through their skill,
seeking health and wholeness
for the weak and ill.

Hear our prayer for surgeons –
experts in their field –
curing and restoring
through the tools they wield;
complex operations
rooting out disease,
mending, curing, changing,
bringing health or ease.

Hear our prayer for nurses,
working on the ward,
caring for their patients;
seeing them restored.
Though their work's demanding
and their shifts are long,
through their ministrations
make their charges strong.

Hear our prayer for patients,
all those being nursed –
some with minor ailments,
some who fear the worst –
battling with worry,
wrestling with pain.
Reach out, Lord, and heal them:
make them well again.

24. Lord, thank you for our senses

Lord, thank you for our senses,
the gifts of scent and touch,
of taste and sight and hearing –
each one that means so much.

We pray for those denied these,
whose senses are impaired;
so undermined or damaged
they cannot be repaired.

For those whose sight is failing
and those who cannot hear –
the future now a challenge –
give strength to persevere.

For those deprived of feeling,
and those who cannot move,
give help to live more fully –
their daily life improve.

For all no longer able
to live as they would do,
give strength, support and succour –
your help to see them through.

25. We pray for those who suffer

We pray for those who suffer
from problems of the mind;
who yearn for help and healing;
who seek but cannot find;
who wrestle with depression
and can't hold back the tears;
who combat inner demons –
a host of unnamed fears.

We pray for those in tumult,
their minds in slow decline,
afflicted by conditions
that cruelly undermine –
so many thoughts that trouble,
that frighten and confuse;
so much we take for granted
that now they stand to lose.

We pray for those who daily
need treatment and support;
their mental health a battle –
a war forever fought.
May counselling and treatment
help all such conflict cease;
bring quietness of spirit –
the joy of inner peace.

26. When summer years have ended

When summer years have ended
and autumn has set in;
when middle age is over
and later years begin;
grant still a sense of purpose,
of all that's yet in store;
the faith that, though it's passing,
life still holds so much more.

When life has changed direction,
assumed a different pace;
no need now for employment;
no children round the place;
grant still a sense of purpose,
of all that we can do;
that though life may be passing,
each day holds something new.

Though health may be declining
and faculties may wane;
though much may prove a challenge
and often bring us pain;
grant still a sense of purpose,
Lord, help us to believe,
life still holds much to welcome
and much still to receive.

27. With love, let us remember

With love, let us remember all those who've lost their health,
a gift so very precious, worth more than untold wealth.
We think of those who suffer, of those oppressed by fear,
of those who each day struggle, and those who shed a tear.

We pray for those with cancer, their future torn apart –
those in the throes of treatment or waiting still to start;
those facing operations or kept alive each day
by drugs or other options that keep the worst at bay.

We think of those whose body continues to be strong,
yet face instead the torment of mind and brain gone wrong;
who wrestle with dementia, or find themselves locked-in,
who struggle with confusion, their life all in a spin.

We think of those disabled in body or in mind,
who have to grapple daily with problems few will find;
whose movement is restricted, whose faculties impaired;
who face a constant challenge that most of us are spared.

We think of those in countries still ravaged by disease;
the deaths of countless children that could be stopped
   with ease;
the deadly epidemics, the countless wasted lives;
all those who wait in torment till help at last arrives.

Reach out to those who suffer; respond to those who cry;
encourage those who worry; encircle those who die.
To all who battle sickness and all who would be whole,
give inner strength and healing in body, mind and soul.

LONELINESS

(*See also* Poverty and human need; Relationships)

28. If you're feeling sad and lonely

If you're feeling sad and lonely,
if you're left out in the cold;
if you long to join the party
but you're kept outside the fold;
think instead of those you're close to,
friends with whom you get along;
think of all you share together
and remember you belong.

If you feel yourself unwelcome,
like a stranger in the crowd;
if you yearn to be accepted
but it feels you're not allowed;
think of parents, partners, siblings –
love so constant, love so strong.
Think of those who count you special
and remember you belong.

If you're not quite sure you matter,
and yet no one seems to care;
if the universe feels empty
and you wonder why you're there;
think again, and know you're precious –
should you question that, you're wrong –
take your place within creation
and remember you belong.

29. No one comes to see them

No one comes to see them,
calls them on the phone;
day by day they sit there,
always on their own.
Someone's feeling lonely,
someone's feeling blue,
hoping for a visit –
will that come from you?

Nothing ever changes,
no one seems to care;
feels like they're forgotten –
is there *no one* there?
Someone's feeling lonely,
someone's feeling blue,
hoping for a phone call –
will that come from you?

One day's like another,
all of them the same:
yearning for a caller –
once more no one came.
Someone's feeling lonely,
someone's feeling blue,
hoping for a letter –
will that come from you?

Feeling quite abandoned,
starved of company.
Nobody to share with,
nobody to see.
Someone's feeling lonely,
someone's feeling blue,
hoping for some friendship –
will that come from you?

LOVING OTHERS

(*See also* Loneliness; Relationships; Service)

30. A group of thieves were waiting

A group of thieves were waiting
as a man came passing by.
They beat him up and robbed him,
then just left him there to die.

'Someone help me! Someone help me!
Will you help in time of need?
Please, I beg you, come and save me!
Won't you do this one good deed?'

A priest came by and saw him;
thought, 'My goodness, I must fly!
I'll be safe if I ignore him' –
so he left him there to die.

A Levite proved as heartless:
for he heard the poor man's cry,
but he hurried off regardless
and just left him there to die.

A third man heard him pleading,
so he stopped to find out why.
When he saw the man was bleeding,
he refused to let him die.

Samaritan and stranger,
he could just have walked on by,
but he put himself in danger
so another didn't die.

'I will help you, gladly help you –
yes, I'll help you out, indeed.
Let me tend you, let me mend you –
be a friend in time of need.'

31. A rich man came seeking

A rich man came seeking, said, 'What must I do
to enter your kingdom above?'
Said Jesus, 'It's simple: no secret involved.
Just follow my teaching on love.

'Reach out to your neighbour – that's all that I ask –
and love them as much as yourself.
Do this and discover, a gift beyond words:
a treasure more priceless than wealth.'

'But who is my neighbour?' the rich man replied.
'I feel that you're just poking fun.
So many live near me, too many to count –
you surely can't mean every one!'

Then Jesus smiled gently, and turned to the man:
'You misunderstand me indeed.
Yes, these are your neighbour, and countless besides:
your neighbour is any in need.'

He speaks still as clearly, as plainly today –
his challenge to me and to you.
To enter God's kingdom, show love here on earth –
express it in all that you do.

32. Are you hungry?

Are you hungry?
Are you needy?
Are you lonely?
Let me share.

Are you hurting?
Are you grieving?
Are you sobbing?
Let me care.

Are you flagging?
Are you wilting?
Are you fading?
Let me care?

Are you doubtful?
Are you fearful?
Are you needful?
Let me care.

Are you quaking?
Are you aching?
Are you breaking?
I'll be there.

33. God gives a new commandment

God gives a new commandment,
and calls us to obey;
to spurn the way of ego
and live another way:
a life concerned with service,
the usual roles reversed –
not seeking *our* advancement
but putting others first.

God gives a new commandment
that nothing comes above;
the whole of what God asks for
is summarised by love:
the call to love our neighbour,
whoever they may be;
to care about their welfare
and serve them faithfully.

God gives a new commandment;
it's simple but it's tough,
for though we try to do so,
we cannot love enough.
Although we meet with failure
and daily go astray,
we need to keep on trying:
there is no other way.

34. In the poor and broken

In the poor and broken,
may we see your face;
consciences awoken
by their wretched case.

In the sick and hungry,
may we hear your call.
May we see your presence
in the plight of all.

In the sad and lonely,
may we see you there.
Help us show commitment
through the way we care.

In our sisters, brothers,
may we feel your touch.
Help us give to others –
we who have so much.

In our love and caring
help us, God, to see,
here is true religion:
what you'd have us be.

35. It's easy to speak about love

It's easy to speak about love,
to say it's what shapes how we live;
to claim that it sets us apart;
and fashions the service we give.
But is this just so many words –
our claims undermined by the facts?
Intentions belied by the way
they fail to be matched by our acts?

It's easy to speak about love,
to say it's what everyone needs.
But does it define who we are
and truly translate into deeds?
Whenever we're put to the test,
does love show itself to be real?
Or is it exposed as a sham –
a vague aspiration we feel?

It's easy to speak about love,
to claim it's the heart of it all –
the word that gives meaning to faith,
the truth that embodies God's call.
Yet what really matters is this:
not just that we're talking the talk,
but, faced with the moment of truth,
we're equally walking the walk.

36. Someone near is hurting

Someone near is hurting,
more than they can bear,
seeking help and comfort,
looking everywhere.
Will you show compassion?
Won't you be aware?
Focus more on others –
show the world you care.

Thousands more are hurting,
tearing out their hair,
overwhelmed by problems,
driven to despair.
Will you show compassion?
Won't you hear their prayer?
Focus more on others –
show the world you care.

Multitudes are hurting,
kitchen cupboards bare:
weak, deprived and starving –
life just isn't fair.
Will you show compassion?
Won't you learn to share?
Focus more on others –
show the world you care.

37. Will you open your hand to the hungry?

Will you open your hand to the hungry?
Will you open your heart to the poor?
Will you open your mind to the lonely?
Will you open your life that bit more?

Will you show that you care about others?
Will you show them they matter to you?
Will you show that your faith's about loving?
Will you show it in all that you do?

Will you give of your time and money?
Will you give of your skills and your wealth?
Will you give of your strength and your vigour?
Will you give what you've kept for yourself?

Will you care for the weak and the needy?
Will you care for those broken by life?
Will you care for the grieving and orphaned?
Will you care for the victims of strife?

Will you open your hand to the hungry?
Will you open your heart to the poor?
Will you open your mind to the lonely?
Will you open your life that bit more?

38. You say that you would love me?

You say that you would love me?
You know then what to do.
If you would show devotion,
then love your neighbour too.

You say that you would love me?
Let's put it to the test:
you care for friends and loved ones,
but what about the rest?

You say that you would love me?
Then this is what I ask:
pour out that love on others;
make that your daily task.

You say that you would love me?
Bring honour to my name?
Then work for peace and justice:
make those your constant aim.

You say that you would love me?
Then prove that claim has worth;
if you would see my kingdom
help build it here on earth.

You say that you would love me?
Do all things for my sake?
Let's see then if you mean it:
what difference does it make?

POVERTY AND HUMAN NEED

(*See also* Social justice; World need)

39. Can you spare a penny?

Can you spare a penny?
Help me buy a crust?
Could you offer something?
Lift me from the dust?
Won't you give a little?
Have you *nothing* spare?
I'm so poor and hungry;
don't you even care?

Can you give assistance?
Won't you ease my plight?
Won't you strive to change things?
Put life's evils right?
Will you work to help me?
Bring redemption near?
Thousands cry for justice;
no one seems to hear.

Can't you give a welcome?
Open up your doors?
We're so tired of running,
fleeing drought and wars.
Won't you help us settle?
Some compassion show?
Life has left us hopeless.
Don't you want to know?

God, I hear your summons
calling out to me.
In the crushed and burdened,
longing to be free.
Needing our commitment,
urging us to share.
In the poor and hungry,
Lord, I meet you there.

40. Do you know what it's like to be lonely?

Do you know what it's like to be lonely?
To have no one you count as a friend?
To spend days by yourself in succession
with no reason to think this will end?
Can you show these they've not been forgotten,
help them know that they're not quite alone?
Can you offer your time and commitment,
so they're not left to cope on their own?

Do you know what it's like to be hungry,
to go day after day without food?
To rely on a handout of rations
for which hundreds of others are queued?
Can you show these they've not been forgotten,
help them know that they're not quite alone?
Can you offer your time and commitment,
so they're not left to cope on their own?

Do you know what it's like to be homeless,
to be left having nowhere to go?
To be far from your friends and your homeland?
To be driven from all that you know?
Can you show these they've not been forgotten,
help them know that they're not quite alone?
Can you offer your time and commitment,
so they're not left to cope on their own?

Do you know what it's like to be needy?
To struggle each day to get through?
To try to provide for your loved ones
when your rent, debts and taxes are due?
Can you show these they've not been forgotten,
help them know that they're not quite alone?
Can you offer your time and commitment,
so they're not left to cope on their own?

41. Do you see the children

Do you see the children,
hunger in their eyes?
Do you hear their pleading,
as another dies?
Do you feel the anguish?
Do you share the pain?
Have you grasped that Jesus
suffers here again?

Have you seen the mother,
thoughts consumed with dread?
Begging for her children,
that they might be fed?
Do you feel the anguish?
Do you share the pain?
Have you grasped that Jesus
suffers here again?

Have you seen the father,
broken by despair,
as his loved ones suffer
more than he can bear?
Do you feel the anguish?
Do you share the pain?
Have you grasped that Jesus
suffers here again?

Have you seen the nations
overwhelmed by drought,
praying for assistance,
aid to help them out?
Do you feel the anguish?
Do you share the pain?
Have you grasped that Jesus
suffers here again?

42. Have you seen the vagrant

Have you seen the vagrant
lying in the street,
asking for some coppers,
desperate to eat?
Did you even notice,
stop to wonder why?
Or did you, as so often,
simply pass on by?

Have you seen the children,
hungry, weak, unwell,
ravaged by starvation,
left to live in hell?
Did you even notice,
stop to wonder why?
Or did you, as so often,
simply pass on by?

Have you seen the stranger,
viciously abused;
judged by creed or colour –
so unfairly used?
Did you even notice,
stop to wonder why?
Or did you, as so often,
simply pass on by?

Have you seen the worker,
hopes and dreams destroyed;
just a bleak statistic:
'long-term unemployed'?
Did you even notice,
stop to wonder why?

Or did you, as so often,
simply pass on by?

Have you seen the nations
left in dire need;
ruthlessly exploited,
victims of our greed?
Did you even notice,
stop to wonder why?
Or did you, as so often,
simply pass on by?

Have you seen the countries,
torn by civil war;
innocents left asking:
'What's the bloodshed for?'?
Did you even notice,
stop to wonder why?
Or did you, as so often,
simply pass on by?

Have you seen God hurting
in this world of pain?
Have you heard him calling,
time and time again?
Did you even notice,
stop to wonder why?
Or did you, as so often,
simply pass on by?

43. Spare a thought for someone

Spare a thought for someone
wrestling with need;
struggling with famine,
desperate to feed;
lacking life's essentials,
starved of basic health –
spare a thought for someone
other than yourself.

Spare a thought for children
shamefully abused;
victims of molesters:
innocence ill-used:
lives once full of promise,
now so cruelly marred –
spare a thought for children
left forever scarred.

Spare a thought for countries
torn apart by war;
people left bewildered,
stunned by 'shock and awe';
thousands maimed and injured,
countless others dead –
spare a thought for victims
of the blood that's shed.

Spare a thought for people
left as refugees;
lacking sanitation,
ravaged by disease;

eking out a living,
getting through the day –
spare a thought for people
forced to live this way.

Spare a thought for nations
crushed by heavy debt;
promised new beginnings,
but, it seems, *not yet*;
tasting just a fraction
of this planet's wealth –
spare a thought for someone
other than yourself.

44. When they turned me from your borders

When they turned me from your borders,
when they said, 'You can't come in';
when my search to find asylum
proved I simply cannot win;
did you even bat an eyelid,
your attention briefly caught?
Do I really count for nothing
but the merest passing thought?

When my children died of hunger
while I watched them writhe in pain;
when the rains were slow in coming,
meaning famine struck again;
did you think about responding?
Did you heed the call to give?
Did you sacrifice a little
so that we might simply live?

When a multitude lay dying
though they could have been made well;
when an epidemic started
and the deaths began to swell;
did you feel a pang of conscience
and respond as best you may,
or with words that count for little
did you simply vow to pray?

When we laboured in a sweatshop,
when we toiled in the fields,
when we staggered with exhaustion,
always pressed for bigger yields,
did you think it was more immoral,
such unfairness rather strange?
Did you heed our cries for justice
and resolve that things must change?

PREJUDICE AND DISCRIMINATION

(*See also* Relationships)

45. The world is cruelly broken

The world is cruelly broken
by prejudice and fear,
by hatred of 'the other'
and all that they hold dear.
Some ridicule and harass;
some publicly condemn;
some close their minds to others –
see only 'us' and 'them'.

A person's sex or gender,
the colour of their skin,
the culture that they come from,
the creed they follow in –
so much that should enrich us
bring bitterness instead –
a world of angry factions
and people seeing red.

Where prejudice is rampant,
where ignorance divides,
where differences estrange us,
entrenching warring sides,
bring openness of spirit,
a softening of views –
the wit to think more deeply
and stand in others' shoes.

46. We claim to be enlightened

We claim to be enlightened,
to welcome people in,
but some are still despised for
the colour of their skin.

We claim to be inclusive,
embracing straight and gay,
but actions all too often
belie the words we say.

We claim to be accepting,
more tolerant of all,
but bigotry and hatred
between us build a wall.

We claim to be more equal,
the gender gap addressed,
but wrongs are still too common
and need to be redressed.

God, may your love and goodness
shape everything we feel.
May openness define us –
unquestionably real.

QUESTIONS OF FAITH

47. I saw a loved one die today

I saw a loved one die today,
they faced such dreadful pain,
and once again, it seemed, O God,
my prayers had been in vain.

Another bomb went off today,
one more atrocity,
more carnage on our city streets –
why do you let it be?

I watched the news in tears today,
appalled by scenes of death,
of famished children, skin and bones,
give up their fight for breath.

So much, it seems, belies our faith,
so little making sense.
It's hard, Lord, not to ask ourselves
if it's just mere pretence.

And yet in all life's tragedies
we still need grounds for hope;
some higher cause in which to trust,
some faith to help us cope.

So when such questions trouble us,
and we can't work them out,
Lord, grant us then, strange though it sounds,
the faith we need to doubt.

48. I try to keep on trusting

I try to keep on trusting
in all that I've believed,
but sometimes, Lord, I wonder
if I've not been deceived.
For much occurs to challenge
and much to horrify,
and then, disturbed and shaken,
I can't help asking 'Why?'

I talk about your goodness –
of how you love and care –
but often, if I'm honest,
you simply don't seem there.
So many seem to suffer,
so many others die,
and then, disturbed and shaken,
I can't help asking 'Why?'

A natural disaster,
a hideous disease,
a war, a drought, a famine,
brings countries to their knees.
So much for countless people
goes hopelessly awry,
and then, disturbed and shaken,
I can't help asking 'Why?'

We try to make a difference,
to change the world for good;
to help the poor and needy
enjoy life as they should.
But nothing seems to alter,

no matter how we try,
and then, disturbed and shaken,
I can't help asking 'Why?'

The wicked seem to prosper,
the good go to the wall;
the way we live appears not
to matter much at all.
Our talk of truth and justice,
life seems to falsify,
and then, disturbed and shaken,
I can't help asking 'Why?'

I can't stop doubts from forming –
so much I want to know.
The questions keep on coming
and will not let me go.
So much, Lord, leaves me puzzled
and seems to mystify,
and then, disturbed and shaken,
I can't help asking 'Why?'

49. The world, it seems, is full of pain

The world, it seems, is full of pain –
relentless tragedy;
so much that you allow, O God,
is just a mystery.

The rich exploit, abuse the poor.
The strong oppress the weak.
This life for some is full of joy;
for others hard and bleak.

For all our talk of doing good
it's evil that holds sway.
We claim there's nothing strong as love,
yet hatred wins the day.

So many weep; so many hurt;
so many groan in pain.
So many die; so many beg,
yet seem to plead in vain.

And though I try to work it out,
I simply cannot see
why you allow such suffering –
how you can let it be.

Day after day, time after time,
once more you crucify.
I try so hard to keep the faith,
yet can't help asking why.

50. We talk of a God who loves us

We talk of a God who loves us,
who in all things works for good.
We speak of a higher purpose –
all proceeding as it should.
We claim that our prayers are answered,
that there's more to life, above.
That though hatred may oppress us,
it can never conquer love.

Yet the world remains divided,
racked by violence and war,
and there's just as much injustice
as there's ever been before.
There's still poverty and hunger,
abject suffering and need.
There's still evil and corruption,
naked cruelty and greed.

Though we pray for new beginnings,
such ills never seem to end.
Though we long to witness healing,
nothing ever seems to mend.
We continue just as broken,
just as held in thrall by wrong,
and our problems seem as pressing
as they have done all along.

Help us, Lord, in all the squalor,
all the pain and all the tears,
all the conflict and injustice,
all the bitterness and fears,
still to see a ray of sunshine,
through the darkness, shafts of light –
signs that, though so much seems hopeless,
you will bring an end to night.

51. Why do you turn away, Lord?

Why do you turn away, Lord?
Why do you not hear our prayer?
Why is our world still broken?
Why do you not seem to care?
Are you no longer active?
Have you been overthrown?
Are you a mere delusion?
Are we just here on our own?

Why do so many suffer?
Why do you leave them in pain?
Why do you leave us grieving?
Why do our prayers seem in vain?
Are you remote, unfeeling,
heedless of what we feel?
Is faith a sad illusion –
none of it actually real?

Though life may bring us trouble,
more than its fair share of woes,
help us to trust despite them
all's not quite as we suppose.
Teach us that though it is hidden,
our pain is *your* pain too,
and though your love is thwarted,
somehow you'll help us get through.

RELATIONSHIPS

(*See also* Loneliness; Loving others;
Prejudice and discrimination)

52. If a friend's in need and you just don't care

If a friend's in need and you just don't care,
if they're in a fix yet you still won't share,
if you only give what you've going spare,
then it's you, I fear, who's in need of prayer.

If you ditch a friend when they're feeling low,
if you're asked to help and you just say no,
if you turn your back when they need you so,
then you're more in need than you'll ever know.

If a friend is stuck and they can't get through,
if you walk away when they're in a stew,
if they find you gone when they're feeling blue,
then you need to ask if your love is true.

Give that extra bit, go that extra mile,
offer what you can with a cheerful smile,
show your faith is real when it's put to trial:
show a loving heart, make it all worthwhile.

53. Let us do to others

Let us do to others
as we'd have them do,
straight in all our dealings,
honest through and through;
swift to show forgiveness,
never self-obsessed;
patient, caring, open;
looking for the best.

Let us love our neighbour –
enemies as well;
care for one another,
serve in ways that tell,
reaching out in friendship,
showing that we care,
constant in a crisis –
simply being there.

Let us live for others,
strive to put them first,
truly seek their welfare
though we come off worst.
If you would more truly
walk a better way,
give and go on giving
freely every day.

54. Stop finding fault with others

Stop finding fault with others.
Stop leaping to condemn.
Don't put on airs and graces
as though it's 'us' and 'them'.
Before you're swift to judgement,
before you cast a stone,
remember that those failings
are just as much your own.

Stop standing on your virtue.
Stop thinking you know best.
Don't think your way is perfect
and never mind the rest.
Respect yourself, most surely,
but learn from others too,
for each and every person
is worth as much as you.

Don't force your views on others,
insisting on your way;
remember truth is often
a murky shade of grey.
Our world is scarred and broken
by narrow-minded views,
by those who, tied to dogma,
deny the right to choose.

Lord, gives us ears to listen,
and eyes that truly see,
and grant a mind so open
we love wholeheartedly,
rebuke our carping spirits,
so swift to criticise;
deliver us from doctrine
that life and love denies.

55. There's nothing quite like laughter

There's nothing quite like laughter
to brighten up the day;
no better way I know of
to chase the blues away.
A daily dose of humour,
a healthy sense of fun,
and soon the clouds are scattered –
we welcome back the sun.

Not laughing *at* another –
a cruel and mocking sneer,
a cold and heartless taunting,
a thoughtless, hurtful jeer;
not teasing without mercy,
nor treating like a fool;
but chuckling together,
amusement shared by all.

To share a joke *with* others –
it does the spirit good,
and saves us from becoming
more solemn than we should.
A world devoid of humour,
how awful that would be.
Let's hear it now for laughter:
come now and smile with me.

56. When I fail to be the person

When I fail to be the person
truly I intend;
when my words and deeds are different –
will you be my friend?

When I'm grumpy, even angry;
when my words offend;
when I'm greedy, mean and selfish –
will you be my friend?

When I've spoken words that hurt you;
words I can't defend;
will you trust I didn't mean them –
will you be my friend?

When I'm silly, careless, thoughtless;
drive you round the bend;
will you see beneath the surface –
will you be my friend?

When I quarrel, cause a break-up
sometimes hard to mend,
will you let me say I'm sorry –
will you be my friend?

When your faith in me is broken,
patience at an end;
though I've let you down so often –
will you be my friend?

57. When someone shows a little act of kindness

When someone shows a little act of kindness,
a little deed of goodness,
a simple sign of warmness,
it's good to show it hasn't gone unnoticed,
that you value what they've done.

When someone shows a little bit of caring,
a little bit of sharing,
concern when you're despairing,
it's good to show your thankfulness, declaring
that you value what they've done.

When someone offers help in times of sorrow,
brings hope to face tomorrow,
gives strength on which to borrow,
it's good to show their gesture wasn't hollow,
that you value what they've done.

When someone gives relief when you are tired,
compassion when required,
support when it's desired,
it's good to show their kindness has inspired,
that you value what they've done.

58. When you're feeling bruised and battered

When you're feeling bruised and battered,
let me be a friend;
let me help, support, sustain you,
faithful to the end.

When you're feeling weak and frightened,
let me be a friend;
there to help you meet the challenge –
strengthen and defend.

When you're feeling spent and weary,
let me be a friend;
let me share the burden with you,
some assistance lend.

When you're feeling lost and lonely,
let me be a friend;
let me show you're not forgotten –
let me love extend.

When you're feeling crushed by sorrow,
let me be a friend;
though your heart feels all but broken,
let me help it mend.

SERVICE

(*See also* Faith in action; Loving others)

59. Can I be of service?

Can I be of service?
Offer some support?
Can I lend a shoulder
when you're falling short?
Can I bear your burden,
help to share the load?
Can I walk beside you;
journey the same road?

Can I show you friendship,
offer love and care;
let you know – whatever –
someone will be there?
Can I make you smile?
Can I make you laugh?
Help to make the sun shine?
Brighten up your path?

Can I share your troubles
when they get on top?
Can I reinforce you
when you're fit to drop?
Can I ease your problems;
help them go away?
Let me be of service;
show me now the way.

60. Can I give assistance?

Can I give assistance?
Help to get things done?
Let us work together:
two instead of one.

Can I share a problem?
Show I understand?
Can I ease your workload?
Let me lend a hand.

Can I offer comfort?
Can I be a friend?
Are you crushed by burdens?
Can I help them end?

Can I make a difference?
If I can, just shout.
Say the word. I'm ready.
Let me help you out.

61. For those who give their money

For those who give their money
and those who use their skill,
for all who have the vision,
the vigour and the will,
to seek to make a difference
and change the world for good,
we thank you, God, and ask you
to use us as you would.

For those who work for justice
and those who strive for peace;
for all who through their actions
see hope and love increase;
for all who offer solace
and seek to ease distress,
we thank you, God, and ask you
their words and deeds to bless.

For those who show compassion
and seek to offer aid;
who strive to heal the broken
and comfort the afraid;
who make the good of others
their overriding aim,
we thank you, God, and ask you
to help us do the same.

62. For those who work to keep us safe

For those who work to keep us safe,
protecting us from crime;
patrol the streets, uphold the law,
regardless of the time;
who sometimes have to risk their lives
as most would never dare;
Lord God, with heartfelt gratitude,
we ask you, 'Hear our prayer.'

For those who work to keep us safe,
protecting us from fire;
who risk their lives to douse the flames
when ours are on the wire;
who, in a jam or accident,
we count on to be there;
Lord God, with heartfelt gratitude,
we ask you, 'Hear our prayer.'

For those who keep our land secure,
from all that would alarm;
who take on terror day by day,
protecting us from harm;
who tackle countless hidden threats
of which we're unaware;
Lord God, with heartfelt gratitude,
we ask you, 'Hear our prayer.'

For all who work to keep us safe
from enemies and war;
who work for peace in other lands –
their mission to restore;
who take on tasks and witness scenes
that few of us could bear;

Lord God, with heartfelt gratitude,
we ask you, 'Hear our prayer.'

For those who work to make us well,
who tend us when we're ill;
for doctors, surgeons, nursing staff –
each healing through their skill.
For all who, in a host of ways,
restore us through their care,
Lord God, with heartfelt gratitude
we ask you, 'Hear our prayer.'

63. If you're hurting

If you're hurting,
if you're grieving –
heart about to break –
let me listen,
let me comfort –
help to heal the ache.
Let me be a friend to you
in your time of need.
Let me show how much I care –
be a friend indeed.

If you're anxious,
if you're troubled,
crying out for peace,
let me offer
reassurance –
help those worries cease.
Let me be a friend to you
in your time of need.
Let me show how much I care –
be a friend indeed.

If you're lonely,
feeling friendless –
seems you're on your own –
let me show you,
though you doubt it,
that you're not alone.
Let me be a friend to you
in your time of need.
Let me show how much I care –
be a friend indeed.

If you're weary,
life a struggle –
health and vigour gone –
let me share the burden with you –
help you carry on.
Let me be a friend to you
in your time of need.
Let me show how much I care –
be a friend indeed.

64. Let us serve one another

Let us serve one another as we ought.
Let us love one another as we're taught.
Let us show we're made new
through the things that we say and do.
Together, he calls us to serve.

Let us serve one another, learn to share.
Let us love one another, show we care.
In the race that we run,
may our words and our deeds be one.
Together, he calls us to serve.

Let us serve one another, day by day.
Let us love one another, come what may.
Through the help that we give
and the way that we're seen to live,
together, he calls us to serve.

65. Will you offer service?

Will you offer service?
Do the loving thing?
Work for truth and justice?
Help the suffering?
Will you make a difference,
putting others first –
changing life for better
where it's at its worst?

Will you offer solace;
comfort those who grieve?
Help the disadvantaged –
penury relieve?
Will you give your money?
Time and talents too?
Bringing hope to others.
Building lives anew.

Will you care more deeply
for a world in need?
Will you not abandon
selfishness and greed?
Millions still are calling,
begging you to hear.
Will you seek God's kingdom –
help to bring it near?

SOCIAL JUSTICE

(*See also* Poverty and human need; World need)

66. A voice is calling, somewhere

A voice is calling, somewhere;
it's crying in despair;
it's poor, and weak, and hungry,
and asking you to share.
It's shattered by disaster;
it's broken by disease.
It feels that there's no future.
It's saying: 'Help me, *please!*'

A voice is crying, somewhere;
it's weeping in despair;
it sees its loved ones dying,
yet no one seems to care.
It speaks of bitter sorrow,
of violence and war.
It's saying, 'Won't you help us?
Spare something for the poor?'

A voice is calling, somewhere;
it's groaning in despair;
it sees such exploitation
and asks us, 'Is this fair?'
The rich grow ever richer,
the poor are left to cope.
They're calling you to listen.
To hear, and give them hope.

67. Falsehoods are spoken

Falsehoods are spoken,
wrong after wrong.
Bodies are broken,
evil seems strong.

Children mistreated –
hurt and abused;
innocence cheated;
kindness refused.

People diminished:
bias still reigns.
Change is unfinished
while it remains.

Workers' rights flouted,
put to the sword.
Dogma is spouted,
justice ignored.

Millions left crying,
hungry and poor.
Thousands more dying,
victims of war.

God, in our darkness,
sorrow and pain,
bleak in its starkness:
shed light again.

68. I hear the sound of bitter weeping

I hear the sound of bitter weeping –
it comes from far away.
It is the sound of broken people,
ignored and tossed away.
Of those exploited, poor and hungry;
of orphan, refugee;
of those caught up in war and bloodshed –
all yearning to break free.

I hear the sound of those despairing –
it comes from somewhere near.
It speaks of hopelessness and hardship,
not far afield, but *here*.
Of homelessness, the unemployed,
the poorly clothed and fed;
of those in debt, in need, in trouble,
who dare not look ahead.

I hear the sound of pain and hurting –
of those who yearn for health.
They're told it costs too much to treat them
despite this planet's wealth.
And so too many still must suffer
while countless others die.
For all our talk of making progress
the world still walks on by.

I hear the cry of angry voices –
they come from all around.
They call for love, for peace, for justice –
an ever-swelling sound.
They plead for change, for something better,
a world with room for all.
A nameless throng seeks new beginnings:
give ear and heed their call.

69. In a world where all too many

In a world where all too many
have no place to lay their head,
grant the will to offer shelter,
giving them a home instead.
May the refugee and migrant
find the help and strength to cope;
through our loving, through our sharing,
may they know there's cause to hope.

In a world where all too many
live each day in crushing need,
eking out a meagre living
while so many pay no heed,
speak your word of truth and justice,
challenge our complacency.
Help us share this world's resources
that we use so shamelessly.

In a world where all too many
feel they do not have a stake,
left dependent on our largesse,
though they give more than they take,
grant the will to make things better,
bringing hope to every race;
help us build a fairer system,
giving all an equal place.

70. In this world of markets

In this world of markets,
global enterprise –
trade the seeming mantra
on which all relies,
hear our prayer for others,
people left behind –
out of sight so often;
also out of mind.

Hear our prayer for workers,
paid a dismal wage;
those employed in sweatshops,
many underage;
victims of recession,
overcome by debt;
unemployed and migrant,
future under threat.

Hear our prayer for people
robbed of work by health;
those who turn to food banks,
'just to feed myself'.
Many who are homeless,
many in despair,
feeling life is hopeless –
nothing for them there.

Where there is injustice,
we must work for change;
economic values
help to rearrange.
Some are getting richer,
others poorer still.
Help us make a difference:
give us, Lord, the will.

71. 'Is there no one there to hold me?'

'Is there no one there to hold me?'
begged the child in despair.
'Won't you stop, and tend, and feed me?
Won't you show me that you care?
Oh, you tell me that I matter,
that you'll make the time to pray,
but will no one make a difference:
make this hunger go away?'

'Is there no one there to help me?'
wept the child in distress.
'Is there no one, from their plenty,
who will give to those with less?
Oh, you tell me that I matter,
that you'll make the time to pray,
but will no one make a difference:
make this squalor go away?'

'Is there no one who will heal me?'
groaned the child in dismay.
'There are drugs and treatments out there:
is there no one who will pay?
Oh, you tell me that I matter,
that you'll make the time to pray,
but will no one make a difference:
make this sickness go away?'

'Is there no one who will save me?'
sobbed the child in defeat.
'Won't you clothe me, house me, aid me;
turn my bitter future sweet?
Oh, you tell me that I matter,
that you'll make the time to pray,

but will no one make a difference:
make this hurting go away?'

'Is there no one who will change things?'
sighed the child in disgust.
'I've heard promises aplenty;
is there no one I can trust?
Oh, you tell me that I matter,
that you'll make the time to pray,
but will no one make a difference:
make injustice go away?'

72. Let us work together

Let us work together.
Let us dare to dream.
Let us strive to make things
different than they seem.
Somehow keep believing
life can be made new.
May that vision fashion
everything we do.

Though so little changes,
so much still the same,
keep conviction burning,
nurse the fragile flame.
Though so many suffer,
though so much is wrong,
fill your heart with purpose;
keep commitment strong.

For as long as hunger
withers human lives;
for as long as justice
never quite arrives;
for as long as darkness
overwhelms the light;
let us challenge evil –
work instead for right.

While the rich and mighty
stamp upon the weak;
while for all too many
what life holds is bleak;
while our world lies broken,
scarred by deep divides;
keep the faith, undaunted –
follow where it guides.

73. Someone in the world is hungry

Someone in the world is hungry,
yet not many seem to care.
Will you be the one to help them?
Do you love enough to share?

Someone in the world is homeless,
far from country, far from friends.
Will you work with those who house them,
see that their dejection ends?

Someone in the world is hurting,
sick and suffering, left to die.
Will you try to ease their burden?
Not just look ... then pass on by.

Someone in the world is needy,
poorer than we'll ever know.
Will you work to end injustice?
Will you let compassion show?

Someone in the world is broken,
tortured, beaten, racked with pain.
Will you work to help protect them –
save them from that fate again?

Someone in this world is always
seeking help in their despair.
Will you be the one to hear them?
Have you truly learnt to share?

74. Someone's anxious, someone's fearful

Someone's anxious, someone's fearful,
burdened by a load of debt;
trying vainly to continue
yet unable not to fret;
what they owe forever growing,
never close to being paid;
all their efforts doomed to failure –
more repayments to be made.

Someone's broken, disadvantaged,
forced to work for little pay –
life a hard and bitter struggle,
getting through another day.
Cut-throat markets squeeze them harder,
always asking that bit more.
Yet for all their toil and effort
still they earn less than before.

Someone's hungry, someone's starving,
someone sees their loved ones die;
so much sorrow, so much anguish,
all because we pass on by.
Though we claim to stand for justice,
though we say such wrongs must end,
will we give and go on giving
so that wounds like these can mend?

Someone's angry, someone's shouting,
urging us to think again;
begging us to work together
for those crushed beneath the strain.
In the poor, the weak, the needy,
we are met by God himself,
calling us to share earth's plenty
so that all may taste its wealth.

75. Think about the things you buy

Think about the things you buy,
the places they are made,
the market forces tied to them,
the fairness of the trade.

Think about what you've consumed,
the lifestyle you've enjoyed.
How much has been sustainable?
How much has been destroyed?

Think about the bargain sales,
so easy to afford.
Were workers' rights upheld in these,
or have they been ignored?

Think about the goods we waste,
so much we throw away.
Could we have kept a few of them
to use another day?

Think about the food we eat,
cosmetics that we wear.
Were creatures harmed in making them?
We surely need to care.

Think about the things you do,
the things you eat and use.
Consider the true cost of them.
Think carefully – then choose.

SORROW AND TROUBLE

(*See also* Disaster, times of; War and peace)

76. For all oppressed by sorrow

For all oppressed by sorrow,
we bring our prayer today –
who search in vain for comfort,
pursue it though they may.
The things that brought them pleasure
now bring them only pain.
Lord, heal the scars within them,
that they may smile again.

To those who mourn a loved one,
each day consumed by grief,
give help to bear the anguish –
bring comfort and relief;
the knowledge that you're with them,
creating life anew;
that in our darkest moments
your love will see us through.

To those whose dreams are broken,
whose hopes have failed to flower,
whose plans have come to nothing,
whose life has proven sour,
give faith that life is never
as bleak as they suppose;
that avenues will open
where other doors may close.

To those gripped by depression
that fills them with despair –
each day a barren wasteland,
each moment hard to bear,
help them to know that one day,
the clouds at last will clear.
The night-time will be over,
and dawn will reappear.

77. For all those facing testing

For all those facing testing
more fierce than we will know;
who every day taste trouble –
a litany of woe;
their future in the balance,
suspended by a thread;
Lord God, support and help them,
and grant them joy instead.

To those who grieve, give comfort.
To those at war, bring peace.
To those oppressed, grant justice –
may exploitation cease.
To weak and sick, bring healing.
To those who starve, give food.
Grant hope to those despairing,
and cheer to those who brood.

Lift loneliness through friendship.
Grant help to those in debt.
To those abused, give closure
and help them to forget.
To all for whom life's journey,
brings turmoil hard to bear,
give help to travel onwards,
assured that you'll be there.

78. For the anxious, fearful

For the anxious, fearful,
crushed by weight of care;
for the sad and tearful –
hear, Lord God, our prayer.

For those facing trouble,
difficult to bear,
lives reduced to rubble –
hear, Lord God, our prayer.

For the sick and ailing,
driven to despair,
flesh and spirit failing –
hear, Lord God, our prayer.

For those robbed of chances –
life just so unfair –
change their circumstances –
hear, Lord God, our prayer.

For those bruised and broken,
doubting you are there,
may new hope be woken –
hear, Lord God, our prayer.

79. For the sick and dying

For the sick and dying,
for the ill and weak,
for the hurting, sighing,
God, your love we seek.

For the tired and aching,
for the sapped and stressed,
for those close to breaking,
grant your strength and rest.

For the sad and tearful,
for the bruised and crushed,
for the lost and fearful,
may the storm be hushed.

For the drained, despairing,
for those beaten down,
for those worn past caring,
turn their lives around.

80. For those for whom the path is steep

For those for whom the path is steep
the road is hard, the way is long,
Lord, grant them help to persevere.
Reach out in love and make them strong.

For those for whom the path is dark,
the road confused, the way not clear,
Lord, grant them help to find their way,
and as they walk, to know you near.

For those for whom the path brings woe,
the road brings tears, the way seems bleak,
give knowledge of your tender love
and grant the comfort that they seek.

For those for whom the path brings hurt,
the road brings gloom, the way brings pain,
reach out to lift them from despair,
and set them on their feet again.

81. No words express sufficiently

No words express sufficiently
the anger and the pain
of losing someone close to us –
not seeing them again.

The shock, the grief, the hopelessness;
the sense of dull despair;
the empty place at every meal –
the one no longer there.

No formula can ease the pain;
no words expunge the grief;
no comforter deny the facts;
no tonic bring relief.

The wounds are raw, they cut too deep;
the hurt is all too real.
For those who mourn there seems no way
to heal the ache they feel.

Lord, in your love, reach out to help,
to hold in your embrace;
to offer strength to those who mourn
in everything they face.

Bind up their wounds, and wipe their tears,
support them through the night,
until at last, in their despair,
they glimpse a chink of light.

82. We greet each day alight with joy

We greet each day alight with joy –
so much for us to share.
For all for whom this life brings tears,
we ask you, hear our prayer.

We greet each day enriched by love,
sustained by those who care.
For all who bear the scars of loss,
we ask you, hear our prayer.

We greet each day well fed and clothed –
few hardships asked to bear.
For those enduring daily need,
we ask you, hear our prayer.

We greet each day in health and strength –
few shadows anywhere.
For those in sickness – weak and frail –
we ask you, hear our prayer.

We greet each day enthralled by much
that makes us stop and stare.
For those no longer moved by life
we ask you, hear our prayer.

We greet each day sustained by hope,
the future seeming fair.
For those who've lost the will to live
we ask you, hear our prayer.

83. Where there's loss – the gall of sorrow

Where there's loss – the gall of sorrow;
where there's heartbreak hard to bear;
where such grief obscures tomorrow,
shrouding all in dull despair;
where the heart is all but broken,
feeling like it cannot mend –
Lord, may hope again be woken,
and the days of darkness end.

When there's nothing but reminders
of the one who meant so much;
when the days forever find us
wishing we could hold and touch;
when no words can ease the torment
that we're feeling deep inside;
when life's bleak, the loss abhorrent;
help us grieve the one who's died.

When our world has been diminished
by the loss of one held dear;
when we feel that life is finished –
nothing left to bring us cheer;
when we're crushed by desolation –
certain that we cannot cope;
grant us, Lord, your consolation;
give us reason still to hope.

WAR AND PEACE

84. Did you spy my tears in the news shot?

Did you spy my tears in the news shot?
Did you glimpse our country's pain,
as attempts to end the fighting
proved once more to be in vain?
Did you see our shattered cities,
or the thousands lying dead?
Did you spot the maimed and injured,
or the multitudes who've fled?

Did you hear my sobs at the bloodshed?
Did you sense my growing fear,
as the battle raged more fiercely
and the threat of death drew near?
Did you hear the bullets whining,
and the wild shriek of shell.
Did you see us cringe and cower,
left to face our private hell.

Will you work and pray for our healing?
Will you strive to bring us peace?
Will you seek to end injustice
so that wars like ours may cease?
In a world of hate and conflict
there's never been needed more
a movement of those committed
to ending the scourge of war.

85. God of every nation

God of every nation,
bid our warfare cease.
Heal our bitter divisions,
help us work towards peace.
Conquer hate and oppression,
end corruption and greed;
banish death and destruction,
war, injustice and need.

Where suspicions divide us,
where our quarrels estrange,
help us seek new beginnings,
somehow bring about change.
Move in spirit among us,
peaceable as a dove;
bind our wounds and unite us,
joined together in love.

86. God of the nations

God of the nations,
come now and mend
all our divisions –
help them to end.

Colour and culture,
dogma and creed,
still come between us –
making us bleed.

Still there is conflict,
people bereft.
Countries lie broken –
anarchy left.

Cities are shattered,
thousands displaced.
Help them to cope with
all that they've faced.

Thousands are slaughtered,
sent to the grave.
Reach out and heal us:
come now to save.

Hatred still festers,
wounds remain raw.
Purge us from evil;
rid us of war.

God of the nations,
make our feuds cease.
Bring us together.
Grant us true peace.

87. Our world is scarred by madness

Our world is scarred by madness,
by violence and fear;
the threat of bomb and bullet
is all too real and near.
For faith has turned to poison,
and truth has turned to lies,
and in the cause of terror
another person dies.

Our world is scarred by hatred,
by those who kill and maim;
who take the lives of others
without a pang of shame.
Too many take religion
and twist it to their end,
and harness it to evil
that no one can defend.

Our world is scarred by sorrow;
it touches every place;
extends to every nation,
each culture, creed and race.
A multitude are hurting,
but still some seek to gain
from making yet more suffer
and adding to their pain.

Our world is scarred by evil,
by peddlers of hate;
they choose their prey at random;
care nothing for their fate.
God, bring an end to chaos,
and make divisions cease.
Put terror's thrall behind us
that all may live in peace.

88. Tell me that you've heard about the tears we've shed

Tell me that you've heard about the tears we've shed.
Tell me that you grieve for all those lying dead.
Show, at least, you sometimes pause to wonder why;
that our anguish hasn't simply passed you by.

Tell me that you yearn to see the bloodshed cease.
Tell me that you'll join with those who work for peace.
Prove you really care about the state we're in;
that the change we long to see may yet begin.

Tell me that you've heard our people's frantic pleas,
Tell me that you've seen the plight of refugees.
Show to those surviving in the combat zone,
that they're not just left abandoned – on their own.

Tell me there's a reason still for looking forward;
that our future hasn't simply been ignored.
Give us hope, in all with which we must contend,
that our wretchedness at last will end.

89. Though we come from different places

Though we come from different places,
though we each have different faces,
though we make up different races –
live in peace.

Though we've different ways of seeing,
though we've different ways of being,
though we argue – disagreeing –
live in peace.

Let us learn to love each other,
seeing all as sister, brother,
let our broken world recover –
live in peace.

In a world that needs repairing,
let us try our hands at sharing,
changing hearts and minds through caring –
live in peace.

90. When tensions are livid, suspicions are strong

When tensions are livid, suspicions are strong,
when views are so fixed that all others seem wrong,
when insults are traded and tempers are raw,
Lord, speak words of wisdom and save us from war.

When hatred is fierce and resentment is deep,
when discord estranges until we could weep,
when nation fears nation and trusts them no more,
Lord, speak words of wisdom and save us from war.

When dogma and doctrine insists on its way,
when terror runs rampant and evil holds sway,
when order is threatened and nothing seems sure,
Lord, speak words of wisdom and save us from war.

When greed and injustice divide and deny,
when those long exploited begin to ask 'Why?',
when voices are raised for the hungry and poor,
Lord, speak words of wisdom and save us from war.

When challenges come that we'd rather not face,
when pressed for resources, for money, for space,
when conflicts of interest are hard to ignore,
Lord, speak words of wisdom and save us from war.

WORLD NEED

(*See also* The environment)

91. For those who wander far from home

For those who wander far from home,
the poor and dispossessed,
the refugee and immigrant,
the broken and oppressed –
for people driven from their lands
by war, by hate, by need,
we ask your help, and pledge to show
our love in word and deed.

For those who work for poor rewards
in sweatshop, factory;
who labour long and hard on goods
that they will never see;
for all whom justice passes by,
who struggle to survive,
give hope, Lord God, of better things:
the chance, one day, to thrive.

For those who yearn for medicine,
a roof above their head,
a drink to quench their aching thirst,
a simple crust of bread,
give help, Lord God, to start again,
to make their dreams come true.
May all for whom the days are hard
find life, at last, made new.

92. In a world of tears and sorrow

In a world of tears and sorrow,
help us spread some cheer;
help us comfort those in turmoil,
strengthen those who fear.

In a world of deep division,
help us work for peace;
may we work towards a time when
hate and bloodshed cease.

In a world of greed and envy,
stacked against the weak,
help us strive for greater fairness –
truth and justice seek.

In a world of pain and sickness,
help us be a friend,
showing love and true compassion –
faithful to the end.

In a world oppressed by darkness,
bring an end to night;
though so much seems wrong and hopeless,
help us shed some light.

93. In a world of trouble

In a world of trouble,
in a world of need,
full of wanton evil,
scarred by rampant greed,
let us strive for justice,
let us play our part:
seek to love our neighbour –
serving from the heart.

In a world of sorrow,
in a world of tears,
wracked by dread and terror,
plagued by nameless fears,
let us offer comfort,
let us show we care –
reaching out to strengthen,
lifting from despair.

In a world of hunger,
in a world of death –
voices pleading vainly
till their dying breath –
let us show compassion,
let us learn to give,
sharing from our plenty,
so that more may live.

In a world of folly,
in a world gone mad –
truth perceived as falsehood,
good construed as bad –
let us turn the tables,
serve as best we may:
let us live for others –
take the better way.

94. In a world where countless people

In a world where countless people
daily starve for want of bread,
give the will to show compassion
that the hungry may be fed.

In a world where countless hundreds
have no place to lay their head,
give the will to offer shelter –
grant to all a home instead.

In a world where countless thousands
find their lives destroyed by war,
give the will to keep believing
better times may lie in store.

In a world where countless millions
face injustice day by day,
give the will to make a difference –
work for change, as best we may.

In a world where countless people
feel they simply cannot cope,
give the will to shape the future;
help us strive to bring them hope.

95. Picture a world without any hatred

Picture a world without any hatred,
think of a world without any war –
people committed to working together,
no longer driven to fight any more.
Picture an end to division and bloodshed,
no more destruction or taking of life.
Nations in harmony, one with another,
peace and consensus where once there was strife.

Picture a world without any hunger,
no more starvation or multitudes dead,
no more despair caused by crisis or famine –
everyone nourished and healthy instead.
Think of the things that we throw away daily;
wasted while millions continue in need.
Pray for a world where the wealthy give freely,
ruled by compassion instead of by greed.

Picture a world without any dogma,
bigoted zealots attached to their creed,
fervent believers for whom faith and doctrine
comes before love shown in thought, word and deed.
Think of a world where religion unites us,
draws us together instead of divides –
doubt understood as a strength, not a weakness;
no one left feeling they need to take sides.

Picture a world without any stigmas,
judgement by gender or culture or race.
Labels and jibes put forever behind us –
no one too frightened to show their true face.
Think of a world where the fact that we're different
helps to enrich us instead of estrange.
Dare to believe we can end our divisions.
Dare to believe in the prospect of change.

96. Someone's weeping, someone's sobbing

Someone's weeping, someone's sobbing,
torn by sorrow, racked by grief,
seeking comfort, consolation,
words of hope to bring relief.
In the anguish that they're facing,
in their darkness and despair.
Reach out, Lord, to offer healing,
show to all how much you care.

Someone's running, someone's fleeing,
vainly searching for a home,
forced by war to leave their country,
day by day condemned to roam.
In the anguish that they're facing,
in their darkness and despair.
Reach out, Lord, to offer healing,
show to all how much you care.

Someone's hungry, someone's starving,
someone's dying, someone's dead;
multitudes condemned to perish,
millions pleading to be fed.
In the anguish that they're facing,
in their darkness and despair.
Reach out, Lord, to offer healing,
show to all how much you care.

Someone's taunted, someone's bullied,
someone's broken, someone's cowed,
all because they're seen as different,
face not fitting with the crowd.
In the anguish that they're facing,
in their darkness and despair.

Reach out, Lord, to offer healing,
show to all how much you care.

Someone's groaning, someone's hurting,
someone's grappling with their pain,
needing help to ease their burden –
gently nurture health again.
In the anguish that they're facing,
in their darkness and despair.
Reach out, Lord, to offer healing,
show to all how much you care.

97. Stop a while and listen

Stop a while and listen,
pause a while and see;
think of this world's troubles –
things that should not be:
poverty and hunger,
misery and pain,
people seeking justice –
doing so in vain.

Stop a while to notice,
pause a while to hear;
think of those who suffer,
those who live in fear.
Think about oppression,
war and refugees:
heed their destitution,
listen to their pleas.

Spare a thought for people
other than yourself.
Think of those who daily
wrestle with their health.
Think about their carers,
those who bring relief.
Think of those in mourning,
wrestling with their grief.

Think about the many
bruised by life and scarred;
all beset by trouble,
each day seeming hard.
Those consumed by worry,
those oppressed by dread;
all whose faith's been shattered –
trust and hopes left dead.

98. Voices are crying

Voices are crying,
calling for succour,
others are sighing,
groaning with pain.
People are broken,
crushed by their burdens,
let hope be woken,
blossom again.

Voices are calling,
seeking a future,
problems appalling
stand in their way.
Famine and warfare,
sickness and hunger.
Grant new beginnings,
bring a new day.

Voices are wailing
yearning for comfort,
people are failing,
weak and diseased.
In all they're feeling,
show them compassion;
bring help and healing –
suffering eased.

Voices are pleading,
begging for justice,
multitudes needing
help to get through.
Grant them assistance,
show you have heard them.
Don't keep your distance,
make the world new.

99. What fate awaits our children?

What fate awaits our children?
What will the future bring?
Will life bring special moments
to make their spirits sing?
Or will the deep divisions
that scar our world today,
estrange us more completely
and pluck such hopes away?

The coming generations –
what heritage is theirs?
A life alight with promise
or choked by weight of cares?
Of meaningful employment –
to each their just reward?
Or mounting exploitation,
no prospects, looking forward?

What fate awaits our loved ones?
What stories will be told?
Will war and hate continue
or better things unfold?
Will climate change be tackled
and terror be no more?
Or will such pressing issues
keep growing, ever more?

Lord, shape this world, we ask you –
in all things work for good.
Give those to come good reason
to look forward, as they should.
Help us to live for others
instead of serving self;
to care more for this planet –
and truly seek its health.

100. Where innocents still suffer

Where innocents still suffer
and hunger stalks the land;
where rampant exploitation
and greed go hand in hand;
where hatred leads to bloodshed,
to violence and war;
reach out, O God, in mercy
and lovingly restore.

Where sickness saps the spirit;
disease brings pain and death;
where life becomes a struggle
with every passing breath;
when injury brings hardship
too testing to ignore;
reach out, O God, in mercy
and lovingly restore.

Where workers are exploited,
denied a fair day's pay;
when debts and life's expenses
just will not go away;
when savings are expended,
yet still there's need of more;
reach out, O God, in mercy
and lovingly restore.

When friendships lie in ruins
and marriage ends in tears;
when children are molested,
their lives now plagued by fears;
when those in whom we trusted
now leave us less than sure;
reach out, O God, in mercy
and lovingly restore.